TRUMP VS. CLINTON

Battle to the
WHITE HOUSE

MATTHEW J. JERRY

TABLE OF CONTENTS

You are reading a program for the 2016 Presidential Election. As a citizen you already have a ticket to the event. But, like any good sporting event, you need a guide to the players and some idea of who they are. *Trump vs. Clinton: Battle for the White House* is here to get you ready for the game.

Both Donald Trump and Hillary Clinton get a thorough introduction. Their background, their lives prior to running for President, and some of the problems popping up on their resumes are discussed. Nothing is hidden so that the players, what they stand for, and their game plans are crystal clear.

This is an election scripted directly from a deviant political science professor. One candidate is closely identified with the establishment. The other is a "self-made" billionaire media star reveling in his status as an outsider. There will be several different themes cropping up during the much anticipated debates: outsider vs. insider; populist vs. establishment; outspoken vs. cautious; big picture vs. policy wonk. Two contrasting styles will crisscross the country looking for votes.

One thing is certain: Americans are voting for contrasting characters and styles, rather than issues. How they get things done will be more important than what they do. Warmups are over and the two contenders for the championship are on the field. Learn something about the players in this race. Grab the popcorn and a cold drink, sit back and watch. It will not be politics as usual.

CHAPTER ONE

MEET THE CANDIDATES

T he 2016 Presidential election cycle has been unusual to say the least. Presidential hopefuls Hillary Clinton and Donald Trump face off in what is promising to be the one of the most bizarre, action-packed, and nasty presidential contests that the country has ever seen.

A year ago, no one predicted that Donald Trump—business man, political outsider and long-time registered Democrat— would win the Republican nomination. In contrast, Mrs. Clinton is following the long standing establishment formula. But even she has a few extra grey hairs, and had to work far harder in the primaries than she expected to secure the Democratic nomination. It's a good time to look ahead and see how the two candidates stack up with just a few weeks until early voting starts in many states.

Trump's campaign is, by far, the most interesting event of the cycle. He was helped by the general weakness of the Republican candidates. Too many Republicans cancelled each other out, appealing to the same portion of the Republican base, and splitting the vote too often. Trump, with brilliant political intuition, positioned himself outside the base, appealing to different groups, taking votes from everyone, rather than splitting them.

Very deftly, Trump capitalized on issues that many voters felt should have been dealt with in the last eight years: the economy, trade, unemployment and immigration. One may not always agree with his solutions, but it seems clear that the primary voters sought new, stronger direction from a fresh voice. From the start, with his choice of issues and methods—town hall meetings, and an in-your-face style—he put his opponents on the defensive. They spent the rest of the primary season trying, unsuccessfully, to catch up.

Discontent is not confined just to Republican voters. Bernie Sanders was able to tap into the same frustration during the Democratic primaries that Trump did on the Republican side. Many Democrats are concerned about the direction that the nation and the economy are going. Sanders' solutions can be attractive to Democratic, middle class and working class voters, squeezed by slow income growth, rising healthcare costs and stagnant productivity growth, while the top earners pull farther ahead.

It's worth noting, however, that to ensure victory in the primaries, Clinton was forced to move left on economic policy in order to blunt Sanders' surging support. Of course, the largesse of the large pool of Democratic super delegates meant that she didn't have to stray too far from a general election strategy. His allowed Clinton to strengthen her support with minorities, showing well in the South and border states, where Democrats tend to be more moderate, while still pulling support in the Northeast and West where Sanders was strong. In the end, this combination proved too much for Bernie Sanders.

Looking at the general election, there are problems and concerns that both candidates will have to face. Trump's antics played well in the primaries, but primary voters are very different from the general electorate. They are more committed and more ideologically driven than the average voter. He will also have to overcome history. Trump is a populist, protest candidate. A protest candidate has never won a US Presidential Election. In some ways, Trump resembles William Jennings Bryan (the populist-supported candidate of the Democrats in 1896, 1900 and 1908—and a loser each time he ran) or Strom Thurmond in 1948.

The last significant protest candidate who received a major party nomination was George McGovern in 1972, who lost to President Nixon in a landslide.

Will Trump have to modify his outlandish image? He tried to do this after sewing up the nomination in May. He began by reaching out to RNC Chair Reince Preibus to set up a fundraising apparatus. He fired his campaign manager who was almost as much of a lightning rod for controversy as he is. He picked a credible nominee for Vice President and he started to work more and more from a script, rather than speaking off the cuff. In the months after the convention Donald Trump's campaign appears to be flailing, with new gaffes and plummeting poll numbers, culminating in the ouster of long time political operative Paul Manafort.

Despite real world problems and voter concern over the sluggish economy, immigration and ongoing government dysfunction, the fall race is shaping up as one of style over substance. With little appetite for actual policy proposals and a coherent discussion of policy differences, Americans will be voting for the candidate they think will be the one to tackle the problems.

CHAPTER TWO

ENTHUSIASM GAP

"Toto, I've a feeling we're not in Kansas anymore ..."
—*Dorothy Boyd*, The Wizard of Oz, *1939*

Voters in the 2016 presidential campaign know what Dorothy felt like. The GOP has long been characterized as the party of staid, country club men but this time around the race just feels *different*. The disgust for the status quo coming from the heartland is real and palpable. This is not your father's Grand Old Party anymore, as Jeb Bush literally found out. On the other side of the political fence, Democrats seem to be fighting for their own identity. Do they want to re-live the salad days of the booming 1990's Clinton economy and political triangulation, or double down on the Obama movement that embraces Big Government, social justice and fighting income inequality?

"Change" is one of the most popular words in the modern political lexicon. Woe to the candidate who seeks to keep things just the way they are. Even candidates who are widely perceived as members of the establishment go through great lengths to frame themselves as outsiders. The Republican field in 2016 was one of the largest in recent memory. It was so large that television had to come up with a "second-tier" debate to keep the number of candidates in debates at a manageable level. Even though the Republican field was stocked with impressive resumes of public service, it was a self-promoting billionaire with exactly zero experience in government who prevailed.

On the flip side, Democrats had only three candidates before the race came down to a binary choice: perhaps the most well-known woman in the world, Hillary Clinton, vs. a social democratic senator. The following is an account of the collision course these two dynamic personalities—Donald Trump and Hillary Clinton—embarked on by declaring their candidacies for the office of President of the United States. They have taken American politics in a direction that it has likely never gone before and may never go back.

In a culture that embraces youth, how ironic that the likely finalists for the general election are well past AARP eligibility. Trump will be 70 on Inauguration Day 2017; Hillary, 69. A newcomer to running for office, Trump made his name in the blood sport that is the Manhattan real estate market. During the 1980s he morphed from a real estate mogul into a full-blown media star. In addition to having a shrewd eye for property development, he proved to be a natural at media manipulation and generating a king's ransom in free publicity. He also learned a lesson in media feuds that would serve him well in his next incarnation: when attacked, attack back harder and more viciously.

While Trump is a newcomer to electoral politics, Mrs. Clinton has been immersed in high stakes office-seeking since her thirties. After redefining the role of a First Lady in the 1990s, Mrs. Clinton has eclipsed Eleanor Roosevelt as the most consequential president's wife in the history of the republic. While her career has been inextricably linked to her husband's, there is a sense that she is running this campaign largely on her own. Will Trump upset the entire political system and change the Republican Party as we know it? Tap your heels, Dorothy. It's going to be a wild ride.

CHAPTER THREE

READY FOR HILLARY

"It's no secret that we're going up against some pretty powerful forces that will do and spend whatever it takes to advance a very different vision for America. But I've spent my life fighting for children, families, and our country. And I'm not stopping now."
—Hillary Clinton, June 13, 2015

That comment is as good as any to sum up Hillary Clinton's perception of the political world around her. She delivered it at a rally on Roosevelt Island, N.Y., to formally launch her presidential campaign. It was a carefully choreographed event with perfect optics—bright summer sun and an ethnically diverse crowd behind her. While projecting a maternal tone addressing her favorite topic of helping children and families, the reference to "powerful forces" advancing a "different version of America" is indicative of a deep paranoia of her political enemies accumulated during a public service career spanning four decades. Mrs. Clinton was already setting up any eventual nominee to be the boogeyman.

Of all the public personalities in modern American culture, few have been dissected, scrutinized and interpreted as much as Hillary Diane Rodham Clinton. The number of books written about her could create a small library. In many ways she has become a political Rorschach Test. The mere mention of her name provokes a strong reaction. Apart from her personality, there has been an ongoing parallel discussion about her political values. Is she a centrist or a left-wing radical? A feminist or an enabler of a womanizer? A sober analysis of her record shows that she is a political chameleon. She is who she needs to be depending on the political currents and eddies of the moment.

While the media has documented all the ways that Hillary is not the most skilled campaigner, she brings a considerable amount of assets to the 2016 race. From the time of President Clinton's ascent in Arkansas politics in the 1970s, Hillary has been the political yin to her husband's yang. The power couple impressed Democratic party power brokers with their intelligence and ambition. The couple's Ivy League degrees were evidence of their intellect. What set them apart was their uncanny ability to engender loyalty among their supporters, create an army of allies at all levels of government, and to raise funds unlike few before them.

Historians and partisans have tried to re-interpret the history of the 1990s. Some on the right have argued that the prosperity of that decade was the result of Reagan-era policies that were given enough time to blossom. Others have said that Speaker Newt Gingrich's *Contract with America* pushed the Clinton White House to embrace ideas like "the era of Big Government is over" (Mr. Clinton's words at the time). However, the Clintons can make a powerful statement in 2016 that resonates with a large section of the electorate that was around during the 90s: the Clinton administration was a time of peace for the United States that included a booming economy and an era of prosperity and stability for many Americans.

While many decisions on candidates are made on speculation, Mrs. Clinton can point to her husband's presidency—an administration for which she was Bill's co-pilot and most influential advisor—as a preview of what a vote for her in 2016 would create.

For all of her public life and especially in the 2016 campaign, Clinton has self-identified as a glass ceiling-smashing feminist. Despite that carefully manicured public image, she is unmistakably one part of a two-headed political machine that includes her husband, the 42nd President of the United States, William Jefferson Clinton. It is a sometimes confusing duality about Hillary's career. While she is undeniably intelligent, capable and ambitious, it is difficult to make the case that she would have soared so high and so far on her own. On its face, this is a toxic fact in the most vocal, liminal feminist circles. In that strident world, women are supposed to succeed with a complete absence of a man greasing the wheels for their careers.

Mrs. Clinton's identity as a political activist goes back to her college days at Wellesley and Yale; however, her time as First Lady of Arkansas and later the United States were formative years that shaped her decision-making processes. Mrs. Clinton saw her husband's first term as Arkansas Governor marred by a stalled agenda that delved into minutia, rather than governing. She and her husband also learned that you can't bring a knife to a gun fight. President Clinton has an analogy: if your opponent is going to hammer you, cut their arm off with a cleaver. Bill Clinton's decision to run for president in 1992 started a chapter in Mrs. Clinton's life that cemented her belief that politics is its own unique form of a back alley knife fight that requires a thick skin and a certain ruthlessness. Almost from the time he announced his candidacy for president, Mr. Clinton was dogged by allegations of womanizing during his time as governor of Arkansas.

Mrs. Clinton departed from the traditional role of the supportive, but seldom heard, wife of a politician facing accusations about his character. Rather, she took an active, even combative role in throwing cold water on the claims. In an infamous appearance alongside her husband on ABC's *Nightline* on March 26, 1992, Mrs. Clinton said, "You know, I'm not sitting here like some little woman standing by my man, like Tammy Wynette. I'm sitting here because I love him, and I respect him, and I honor what he's been through and what we've been through together. And you know, if that's not enough for people, then heck, don't vote for him."

Mr. Clinton's polished speaking style and connection with audiences overcame the allegations and carried him into office in January 1993. While the Clinton presidency had its accomplishments, including a soaring economy and relative stability around the world, it is also remembered for the astonishing scandal involving White House intern Monica Lewinsky's sexual affair with the president that led to President Clinton's impeachment. Mrs. Clinton again took on the role of vocal advocate of the president. Before Mr. Clinton admitted to the illicit affair, Mrs. Clinton famously went on television and blamed the scandal on a "vast, right-wing conspiracy." Her examples were – in her opinion – legion.

Conservatives continually tried to make hay out of what the Clintons view as unrelated and irrelevant. A few months after President Clinton was elected as Arkansas Attorney General Mrs. Clinton joined the prestigious Rose Law firm in Little Rock, muddying the waters and blurring the lines between back scratching and Mrs. Clinton's legitimate abilities. This has been an ongoing theme dogging the Clintons over the years, from Little Rock to the White House (the Lincoln Bedroom scandal) and now to the Clinton Foundation.

Some of the Clinton's other dealings that raised eyebrows were Mrs. Clinton's trading on cattle futures contracts, where she invested $1,000 and parlayed that into a whopping $100,000 dividend after just ten months. Later, investment analysts would say that the odds of turning that kind of profit on such an investment are astronomical. It was also during the Little Rock years that the couple made a regrettable decision to invest in the Whitewater Development Corporation, a move that would turn into a public relations nightmare for the couple in later years.

It is true that Mrs. Clinton re-shaped the role of First Lady. No longer just a figurehead for charitable works, she was knee-deep in the trenches of partisan politics. President Clinton asked her to lead developing a proposal for the first incarnation of Obamacare shortly after coming into office. Both Mrs. Clinton and the President were pilloried for the attempt.

Her perception that she and her husband were under constant attack throughout the administrations caused her to close ranks, allowing only a few of the most loyal supporters on the inside. This man-made cocoon traverses the gulf from public to private lives, causing countless headaches for the couple, as appearances of impropriety gather more and more steam.

What does Mrs. Clinton seek for America as she campaigns to become the first female president? There is certainly a body of work to answer that question, based on her time as senator from New York and later as Secretary of State under President Barack Obama. However, her political philosophies appear malleable based on what is popular with the Democratic Party base at the moment. During her time in the Senate, Mrs. Clinton joined with many other Democrats to vote in favor of military action against Iraq. When the war started going badly and the Democrats seized upon it as a campaign issue, she again joined other Democrats in becoming decidedly anti-war.

Similarly, she had maintained a position in those years that marriage is restricted to a union between a man and a woman. In the subsequent years, her party moved leftward (or mainstream depending on which polls you look at) on the marriage issue and Hillary followed suit by modifying her platform to support gay marriage. Is this flip-flopping or being flexible enough to adapt with the times? Or do these apparent flip-flops actual denote an evolving view of societal norms?

Within the confines of Democratic primaries, it does not seem to have hurt her in 2016 as coming around to the correct position in the eyes of the base is more important than having been wrong in the past. It remains to be seen how her changing positions will be received by an electorate that includes independents and conservatives as well as committed liberals.

What does that mean? It explains why he donated money to the Clinton Foundation. It explains why he gave money to Harry Reid. It explains why he has taken opposing positions on myriad issues. Inside the Beltway, message discipline is a prized and admired quality. Those who maintain it often have terms like "reliable conservative" and "lion of the Senate" applied to them. The political media loves nothing more than to have a politician in the studio, have him explain his support or opposition to a proposal and—gotcha!—play a video clip of the same candidate taking the opposite position. The late Tim Russert, one of the most admired interviewers in the political media, made a career out of this tactic as the host of "Meet the Press."

Businessmen like Trump operate altogether differently. Message discipline is still extremely important (i.e branding), but it can be more fungible than traditional political messaging. Company chiefs have one goal and one goal only: to advance the interests of their company. They most likely have core beliefs and a particular world view, but such concerns are secondary in the business world. This concept is even more important in the world of New York City politics. Want to get approval to develop a parcel of land into a five-star hotel? You'll need to curry favor with the City Council, the mayor, the governor, and probably a congressman here and a senator there. How does one accomplish that? Campaign contributions are a good start. If you have conservative beliefs, you'll need to stifle them in a one-party city where Democrats rule the kingdom. This is the world in which Donald Trump made his bones.

During his ascent as a real estate potentate and a media colossus, Trump also developed a carefully constructed public image as a tough guy, a self-promoting Energizer bunny and a problem-solver that has influenced the political positions he advocates today as a presidential candidate. Is it really him or is it just schtick? Does it really matter? Trump Tower isn't just a Manhattan high-rise, it's the greatest building in the world! Rosie O'Donnell isn't just an uninformed know-it-all, she's a "fat pig!" "The Apprentice" isn't just a reality show, it's the greatest, most successful reality in the history of television! You get the picture.

From there it's a short hop to a populist political philosophy. China isn't just becoming an economic power, they're "killing us" and stealing our jobs. Trump isn't just going to stop the flow of illegal immigrants, he's going to build a huge wall on the southern border—and Mexico is going to pay for it! America isn't just going to start winning, we're going to get tired of winning so much! The intelligentsia in the Northeast corridor may cringe at such bombast, but large swaths of people in flyover country, those not living in urban centers on either coast, are swooning.

Another common thread behind every successful presidential campaign is timing. What works in one electoral cycle might be a disaster in another. Jimmy Carter's plain-spoken Southern manner and his pledge never to lie to the public might seem overly folksy and naive today, but it was exactly what many Americans wanted to hear after the protracted ethical swamp that was Watergate. Similarly, many voters today see Trump as the elixir to a political system in Washington that has veered far off its intended course.

In a different electoral season, a candidate who mocked a Vietnam POW for getting caught, called all illegal immigrants from Mexico rapists, criticized a female presidential rival for her appearance, etc. would have been politically radioactive by now. Trump did all those things and not only survived, but grew stronger throughout the primary season as the pundit class incorrectly declared his campaign dead after each incident. Trump's Teflon can be attributed to an unprecedented level of voter resentment at Washington. To his supporters' eyes, Trump's lack of polish is not evidence of his unsuitability for higher office, but rather proof of his outsider status.

For decades now the electorate has grown weary of candidates who have obviously gone through extensive media training on how to speak in safe sound bites that say nothing and commit to nothing. Trump enters that glass shop like an angry bull. Breaking all the conventional wisdom, Trump's words are clearly not tested with focus groups or crafted to please everyone. That kind of honesty has appeal to people who may not even support what is being said.

If you were to ask a typical Trump supporter what specifically they like about his policies on fixing the Middle East, that person would likely not be able to answer in detail. It would not be due to ignorance on that person's part. Trump has steered away from specifics. Confidence in the candidate has come largely from the sheer force of his personality, honed by years of media coverage and his presence in America's living rooms as a reality television star. ISIS is wreaking havoc in the Middle East? Trump will bomb them back to the Stone Age! The details don't matter to most people at this point. The attitude is the thing.

Trump's success thus far also owes itself in part to its lack of commitment to traditional Republican positions. One of his opponents' favorite lines of attack against him has been that he is not a real Republican, nor a real conservative. While Trump has contested the claim, this view allowed him to draw a larger pool of support than a rock-ribbed conservative. After more than seven years of playing the role of the Washington Generals to President Obama's Harlem Globetrotters, the GOP brand is suffering from an identity crisis.

Many on the right argue that the party has allowed itself to be defined by the Democrats for far too long. Republicans are inept at responding to the accusations that they are racist, sexist homophobes who want to throw grandmothers off a cliff and light their cigars with $100 bills. Trump has largely flown over and above such attacks. How can the Democrats frame him as just another clueless Republican when he attacks the decision to invade Iraq and criticizes the trade deals of both Obama and George W. Bush? Trump has been accused of being many things, but he can never be accused of being boring.

CHAPTER FIVE

STYLE VS. SUBSTANCE

In an American culture where reality shows are one of the most popular forms of entertainment, political debates have evolved—or is it devolved?—into their own reality show format. Up until the Television Age, debates were generally a substantive discussion of issues among the candidates and the voters decided which nominee had the soundest proposals. The 1960 election changed everything. It was the first campaign in which television was a major factor. Now debates are largely remembered for who delivered the best sound byte or made a gaffe that threatened to scuttle their whole campaign.

What Senator John F. Kennedy lacked in experience and gravitas in the 1960 campaign, he more than made up for with his good looks and telegenic speaking style. The visual contrast between the two candidates could not have been more stark. Not surprisingly, a majority of voters who watched the debate on television thought Kennedy had won. The radio audience, with only the words of the candidates to define them, thought Nixon won. It didn't matter. Politics and television were inextricably married and still are to this day. Kennedy helped to usher in a new era where campaigns are won and lost in the voters' living rooms rather than packed rallies.

Much like Presidents Kennedy and Nixon, the two party lead dogs today have divergent skills when it comes to the essential medium. Donald Trump is a candidate made for television. Trump has spent most of his career in front of television cameras. Not only is he the CEO of the Trump Corporation, he has also been its de facto public relations director. A lifetime spent in the media capital of the world has given Trump an uncanny sense of how the media operates and how to deliver a message. The media, always looking to cover the sensational and flamboyant can't stop covering him.

Those who have followed Trump's career are no doubt familiar with his speaking style. The world of politics was not ready for what hit them when he declared his campaign. The conventional wisdom of politics is to say a lot without saying much at all. In other words, say something that will get coverage without being controversial or committing to things for which you may later be held accountable. Trump smashed that idea right out of the gate, describing illegal immigrant coming across the southern border as "rapists." So much for conventional wisdom.

In the early Republican debates, Trump garnered attention but was still dismissed by many as a flashy lightweight. By staking out bold positions on immigration, trade and the military, Trump created a template that left the other candidates trying to catch up with his rhetoric. It also became quickly apparent that Trump was bulletproof to the traditional political attack strategies. In Republican politics, there are few more damaging accusations than that a candidate is not a real conservative. The base has come to loathe the Republican in Name Only (RINO), so his opponents assumed that charge would dismiss Trump in short order. There was plenty of evidence supporting the accusation.

As a wealthy businessman, his donations were coveted by politicians from both parties. He had given money to Chuck Schumer, Harry Reid and—gasp!—the Clinton Foundation. He invited the Clintons to his wedding. In an ordinary political season, such facts would doom a Republican candidate. But voter anger and the image of him as the antidote to politics as usual was more than enough to compensate.

One of the most frequent complaints of recent Republican candidates is that they do not defend themselves against attacks. George W. Bush had record approval ratings after the September 11 attacks, but by the end of his presidency he was radioactive. Why? There were many reasons, chief among them was his fateful decision to depose Saddam Hussein and create an open-ended military commitment in a country teeming with jihadists and Saddam dead-enders. Others would argue that what doomed Bush was his refusal to fight back against a relentless barrage of attacks from Democrats.

George W. Bush's *eminence grise,* Karl Rove, admitted that the administration made a conscious decision not to respond to attacks, in part because Bush felt the office of the presidency was above getting in the mud with such unseemliness. The withering assault from the Reid/Schumer/Pelosi troika on Capitol Hill, combined with cooperation from those in news and entertainment, succeeded in driving Bush's negatives to toxic heights. If only he had fought back, many supporters wonder. It is both and indictment of Bush and a compliment in that he was too classy to get down and dirty.

Donald J. Trump has no such affliction. Despite his tailored suites and much-discussed hair, Trump is a street fighter at heart. Say a disparaging word about him on a debate stage and it will be thrown back at you tenfold. Mock his appearance and he will zero in on your least flattering characteristic and make it the main topic of tomorrow's morning talk shows. During the second Republican debate at the Reagan Presidential Library, Trump and Senator Rand Paul were trading punches when a moderator asked Trump why he had criticized Paul's appearance. Trump's response? "I never attacked him on his looks, and believe me there is plenty of subject matter right there," drawing big laughs in the press area. When it became clear that Trump was a real player in the primary, Governors Christie and Bush, and eventually Senators Cruz and Rubio attempted to stand toe-to-toe with Mr. Trump. Although they managed to score points, polling and primary results suggest that they did as less damage to him than they did to themselves. Mr. Trump is a natural showman was able to swat them away like gnats.

Mrs. Clinton is not a natural politician. She cannot tell supporters that she feels their pain and sound convincing. She has carved out her identity as a policy wonk, someone who can consume a stack of briefing books and be able to cite statistics and bill language verbatim. Despite her ambitions, she has found coming across well on television is a difficult skill to master. The more she tries to look and sound authentic on television, the more it tends to look forced and scripted.

In an ironic twist, Mrs. Clinton's public persona most closely resembles that of the left's *bete noire*: President Nixon. Many of the qualities Democrats despised about Mr. Nixon—stiffness, paranoia, poor communications skills—are easily applicable to Mrs. Clinton. Luckily for her, Mrs. Clinton entered the 2016 campaign with more than enough big-donor cash and political machinery to compensate for her perceived lack of warmth. Deploying that political machinery to her advantage will play to her political organizing strengths.

Luckily for her, getting elected President of the United States in 2016 requires a lot more than just personal charisma. It requires a ground game of loyal staffers and volunteers with the skill and ambition to conduct get-out-the-vote campaigns in key swing states. It requires approximately $2 billion for advertising, polling, opening up field offices and other campaign-related expenses. On these counts Hillary is dominant. From her time as First Lady of Arkansas all the way up to her tenure of Secretary of State, Mrs. Clinton has created a vast network of loyalists who have become members of Congress, senators and governors. As residents of New York state and a former First Couple, they have deep ties to Wall Street.

Even though such relationships are considered poisonous by much of the electorate, having allies in the financial capital of the world is necessary to raise the type of money that's needed to win a modern campaign. The Clintons also have a foothold in left-leaning Hollywood, where allies like George Clooney, Jeffrey Katzenberg and Steven Spielberg are a phone call away and more than happy to arrange $30,000-a-plate fundraisers to keep the Clinton campaign war chest full. Mrs. Clinton routinely visits the California ATM machine and connects with her core supporters.

Perhaps the biggest factor in Clinton's favor this time around is the lack of quality competition within the party. While Sanders proved to be skilled in generating millennial support on the left, he presented Mrs. Clinton with only one real primary opponent in a process that traditionally attracts multiple aspirants. In 2008 she had the misfortune of going up against a green but charismatic junior senator from Illinois who launched an improbable campaign but soon caught fire once he was judged to be a "historic" candidate. Hillary had hoped to use the idea of the first woman president as a catapult to propel her into the Oval Office. The Democratic base had other ideas, as Mr.

Obama's campaign built a massive level of hope among the Democratic faithful and independents that propelled him into office.

This time the landscape is very different. There is no historic young candidate to stand in her way. Former Maryland Governor Martin O'Malley had hoped to play that role, but he failed to gain any traction and his campaign barely moved the needle. All that remained was Senator Bernie Sanders from Vermont. Surely this was a situation tailor-made for Mrs. Clinton's ascendency. One of the perceptions of Hillary was that, at age 69 and a longtime Washington operator, she might be considered too old to seek the presidency. The septuagenarian Sanders made her look young by comparison. Sanders' loud and proud identity as a socialist would also make her look more moderate and sensible, which could only help her once the general election campaign began. Sanders is a transplant to Vermont by way of New York City, and his distinctly New York accent made him look more like a regional candidate than a national one. The only thing Mrs. Clinton could have asked for more was to run unopposed.

The Clinton-Sanders debates were notable for two things: their scarcity and their lack of combativeness compared to the GOP debates. Clinton critics were quick to notice that the debates were held at times that seemed to get the smallest audience possible, presumably to hide her flaws as a candidate. One debate heading into the Iowa caucuses was held on a Saturday night opposite assuring a paltry Nielsen rating. Democratic National Committee Chair Debbie Wasserman Schultz (who recently resigned her position) controlled the debates and was an active supporter of Senator Clinton, so it was quickly surmised that she was doing her best to help Mrs. Clinton. It was only after Sanders began gaining traction that Wasserman Schultz suddenly began scheduling more debates.

Noticeable in the debates was Sanders' inexplicable reluctance to go after Mrs. Clinton on her accumulated political baggage. After Sanders proclaimed, "I tired of hearing about her damn emails," Mrs. Clinton must have been ecstatic. He had taken the most damaging issue to her off the table. It was at that point that some in the pundit class started wondering how much Sanders really wanted to win. With a popular but seemingly toothless opponent, a super delegate system that favored her and a bloody civil war taking place in the GOP, the sky was bright for the Clinton campaign. It was not far-fetched to see the Clintons make some presidential history of their own. Not only the first woman president, but the first husband and wife to BOTH be president. The email scandal, Benghazi and the

Clinton Foundation appeared to be in remission. Fortune was finally going to smile on Hillary.

CHAPTER SIX

OPPOSITION RESEARCH

Mr. Trump and Mrs. Clinton are two of the most well-known individuals to run for President. Who else would come close? In 1960 Richard Nixon was the sitting vice president, but the now iconic JFK was a callow young senator who was still creating his public persona. In the modern era of politics, there is much to be gained from having a thin resume. The Robert Bork confirmation hearings in 1988 show why. In 2008 Barack Obama used his lack of experience as an asset. Framing himself as an inspirational leader, Obama tapped into people's hopes and expectations of what he *could* do much more than what he had already done.

Such a candidate can create what is often referred to as a political equivalent of a Rorschach Test. If voters wanted a President who would right the scales of justice in society, he could be that. Never mind that his biography showed no tangible results on that score. His rhetoric was soaring, and his supporters were more than happy to go along for the ride.

There will be no such speculation this time around. Both Trump and Clinton have been public figures since the dawn of the Reagan administration. "Opposition research" is a polite term in the campaign business that refers to digging up dirt on one's opponent. Often campaigns employ vast teams of aides to travel to an opponent's hometown, interview those slighted by said opponent, and craft the best way to exploit that information. With Trump and Clinton, opposition research can be done with access to Wikipedia and TMZ.

In terms of political baggage, there may not be a presidential candidate with more than Mrs. Clinton. To her supporters, she and her husband have been in the crosshairs of the "vast, right-wing conspiracy" since her husband held state office in Arkansas. His ascent to the presidency in 1992 only intensified the animus against them. To their detractors, the Clintons have lived in an ethical swamp for decades. Along the way, they have become multi-millionaires by trading the prestige of their public offices to the highest bidder.

It is ironic that Hillary cut her political teeth in 1974 as a member of the impeachment inquiry staff advising the House Committee of the Judiciary during the Watergate scandal. It is ironic because in their own political careers, both Mr. and Mrs. Clinton have had the suffix "-gate" attached to more of their own scandals than most Americans can even remember. A Google search brings up a staggering list: Filegate, Cattlegate, Travelgate, Snipergate, Whitewater-gate and Email-gate are just a few.

Among her political rivals from both parties, the subject of Mrs. Clinton's scandals has mysteriously been off limits, particularly those involving Mr. Clinton's philandering. It is not fair, her advocates say, to hold the wife responsible for the shortcomings of the husband. For a long time that was an effective argument, but that may be changing. In this election cycle Hillary took a swipe at Trump, suggesting that his language is often sexist. Most Republican candidates would run in fear from a charge like that. The idea of being tagged with the "sexist" label would bring a predictable run of apologies and staged events with a devoted wife insisting that he's really a great guy. How did Trump respond?

"She's not a victim. She was an enabler," Trump said in an interview on Fox News Sunday. "She worked with him. She was –

some of the women have been totally destroyed.
Some of these women have been destroyed.
And Hillary worked with him. "

This represented a shifting of the tectonic plates in terms of how candidates deal with Mrs. Clinton. And what was her reaction? The campaign dropped the matter summarily and seemed in a hurry to talk about anything else. You can bet the farm that Trump will bring up the topic again in one of the debates this fall.

While the '90s-era scandals may still be in play, they are likely to take a back seat to those of the current generation like the email server scandal and the Clinton Foundation's woes. FBI Director James Comey publicly stated that she will not be prosecuted however, he took great pains to point out that Mrs. Clinton was reckless and showed poor judgment. While she has dismissed the case as little more than a "security review," the reality is that she is in extreme legal peril for her decision to set up a private server for government work, send and received documents later determined to be classified, and possibly lying about it to investigators. At this time, there is a House Committee investigating whether or not she perjured herself as more emails continue to trickle in.

Mr. Trump will also likely exploit Clinton Foundation activities. In the aftermath of his presidency, the newly-minted ex-president threw himself into the work of helping the less fortunate around the world, and the vehicle for that was the Bill, Hillary and Chelsea Clinton Foundation. The former First Couple received voluminous positive media coverage for the Foundation's works, and the Clintons' vast network of well-heeled donors are counted on to contribute. What happened after that is subject to interpretation, but the appearance is that there was co-mingling of money between donations and speaking fees that will make great fodder for campaign commercials for the Republican opponent willing to exploit it.

Similarly, Team Hillary's biggest challenge may not be finding usable opposition research on Mr. Trump, but selecting the best themes from a cornucopia of options. More recently, Mr. Trump's campaign announcement included rhetoric that will allow Mrs. Clinton to scare Latinos ("they're rapists"), a demographic coveted by both parties. Trump's promise to build a wall on the southern border—easily the most popular pledge at his rallies—is sure to be exploited by the Democrats as evidence that Trump is anti-Hispanic. Will Trump make the obvious reply, that curbing illegal immigration will also serve to help Hispanic Americans to find better jobs, make more pay and generally be safer? It's anybody's guess.

Trump's decades of business dealings are also sure to come up. The Obama re-election campaign had great success with a TV spot featuring a factory worker with a sad tale of how his wife died of cancer after a facility run by Mitt Romney's corporate turnaround company was shut down. Was Romney responsible for the woman's death? Not really, but American culture has regressed to the point where being guilty or innocent isn't nearly as important as being perceived as a nice guy, and the ad convinced many voters that Mr. Romney was not a nice guy.

Already a New Jersey woman has been identified as a victim of Trump's eminent domain efforts to develop parcels in Atlantic City. Expect that woman to be a Warhol-like, 15-minute celebrity during the fall campaign. The bankruptcy filings of Trump's companies are also sure to come up. Trump's biggest claim to fame—that he is a business genius with a Midas touch—is likely to come under harsh attack by a Democrat campaign machine that relishes painting its GOP opponents as heartless plutocrats who are hopelessly out of touch with the problems of the middle class.

The recent news that the Russian government hacked into the Democratic National Committee's computers and accessed their opposition research on Trump was not surprising, in that it didn't reveal anything new about Trump. However, it did confirm some of the strategies that many suspected. Namely, that the Clinton campaign would emphasize Trump's actions and statements to frame him as a misogynist who is no friend to women. His two divorces, his first wife's <u>claim</u> (later retracted) that he raped her, and a seemingly endless list of boorish comments about women will all play into the Clinton campaign's narrative of her opponent. That tactic, coupled with Mrs. Clinton's framing of herself as a historic first female president, is apparently the plan to keep a traditionally reliable Democrat voting bloc—women—in the fold.

Trump's tendency to make his public appearances look like stream of consciousness ramblings play into another Clinton narrative, namely that Trump lacks the temperament to be president and would destroy America's standing in the world and at worst start a global war. Trump's lack of a track record in government fuels this idea. If he is a bombastic, politically incorrect bull in a china shop, what on Earth would he do once in control of the levers of government? His statements about the judge in the Trump University case, specifically that a judge of Mexican descent couldn't possibly give him a fair hearing, are political correctness taken to the extreme and are likely to alienate members of a voting group for which Trump claims he will find electoral success.

More likely, Mrs. Clinton is likely to dust off the Obama Campaign strategy that worked so well against Romney. Expect Trump to be depicted as a greedy, cold-blooded real estate baron. That narrative may be Mrs. Clinton's best shot to win over the millennial Sanders supporters who have considered her an avatar of the one percent in bed with the big banks.

If you are seeking a political dialogue where there are substantive policy debates and two competing visions of what government is…this is not your election. The mud will be flying at a record clip.

CHAPTER SEVEN

WHAT'S AT STAKE

The political talking heads often say, "This is the most important presidential election in the nation's history." The 2008 election was the "most important" because the nation stood on the precipice of electing its first African-American president. The 2000 election was described similarly because it represented a fork in the road between the Clinton presidency and an alternate path. A case can easily be made that every election of the moment is absolutely imperative to the country's future.

That said, it may not be hyperbole to apply that description to the 2016 contest. Why? Quite simply, it may be the biggest potential course correction in modern times. Even the most liberal and ardent Obama defender would concede that he has certainly taken the country in a leftward direction.

The results of the Obama presidency are open to interpretation depending on where you fall on the ideological spectrum. To many on the center-left, the Obama Administration has been a golden age that ushered in greater tolerance and diversity as relates to minority groups; a different global footprint and posture after what many described as the "cowboy diplomacy" of George W. Bush; a commitment to renewable energy and a dressing down of Big Oil; and the implementation of the left's most sought-after goal: universal health care. The idea of losing those accomplishments to an incoming Republican administration is ample motivation for most Democrats to get themselves to the polling station in November.

On the other side, motivation to vote is in abundant supply. To anyone with conservative leanings, the Obama Administration has been nothing short of a nightmare. Every item on the extreme left's wish list seems to have been implemented. America has abdicated its role as the only global superpower as bad actors like Iran, China, and Russia have made aggressive moves they never would have previously dreamed of. Our sovereignty has been weakened by this Administration's open-borders immigration policy, which has also resulted in the continued balkanization of American culture.

Big Government spending has caused an already bloated national debt to grow to unthinkable levels. The idea of the first African-American president serving to heal racial divides has produced the exact opposite effect: few can recall a time in their lives when there was this much racial polarization. To people of this view, nothing short of the country's existence is hanging in the balance with this year's election result.

There is one caveat to all this political gamesmanship. Usually around convention time, the parties each settle on their nominees, and the faithful begin to rally around that candidate and present a unified front for the fall campaign. This is another reason why this year is unlike few before it. Within each party are rifts so deep that the idea of total unification behind the nominee is highly unlikely.

The Republican primary campaign made for some of the most riveting dramas on television. A huge field early on, with a well-known reality TV star and insult-filled debates made the GOP America's favorite train wreck to watch. The biggest feud within the party has been the struggle between "the establishment" and "the outsiders" for control of the party. Casual political observers who think the GOP is a monolithic party could not be more mistaken.

The establishment, with control of the GOP apparatus in Washington, has mostly had their way in the party since Ronald Reagan's presidency ended in January 1989. Since then, the offerings for president have tended to be safe, moderate types that would not rock the boat and offered more of the same. More right-wing elements of the party would say that selecting these vanilla candidates resulted in handing President Clinton a second term and President Obama another two.

Determined not to go into another presidential campaign with a dead-on-arrival candidate, the conservative base's anti-establishment ethos was stronger than ever this time around. Unlike some years when only one candidate was running a Quixote-like protest candidacy against the system, 2016 offered several legitimate outside candidates. Senator Ted Cruz of Texas has been a far right, conservative favorite since coming to Washington. With his Ivy League sheepskins, impressive debating skills and impeccable conservative credentials, he embodied the purest conservative since Reagan to seek the Oval Office. Wisconsin Governor Scott Walker took on the big unions in his state and won every time. A newcomer to the national stage, he nonetheless possessed the backbone and the brains to take on the entrenched left.

Then there was Trump. His highly confrontational — some would call it juvenile—campaign style helped create extreme reactions to him. Those who liked him would look the other way at his outrageous statements and name-calling, wait in huge lines to get into his rallies and fight back against protesters looking to disrupt his events. That kind of passion resulted in supporters claiming they would never back another candidate. In response, others formed the "Never Trump" movement, an organized mechanism of the establishment to derail Trump.

While Trump raced out to a big delegate lead, Cruz stayed within striking distance. Ohio Governor John Kasich stayed in the race amid calls to drop out because of losses in all but his home state. As Cruz got closer with a win in Wisconsin, talk of a contested convention grew louder. The Republican base seethed as the media reported that the establishment was plotting to deny Trump the nomination and even try to install one of their favorites, such as moderate Speaker of the House Paul Ryan, as the nominee despite the fact that he didn't run at all in the primaries.

Trump and Cruz behaved like allies early in the primary season. Once Cruz started winning states, Trump began a scorched-earth campaign that referred to Cruz as "Lyin' Ted" and started an ugly Twitter war that involved the candidates' wives. The idea that these two remaining serious candidates—or their supporters—could create party unity with so much bad blood in the primaries seemed remote. At the Republican Convention Sen. Cruz refused to endorse Mr. Trump and was booed off the stage. Add Gov. Kasich's refusal to assist Mr. Trumps campaign in Ohio – a key swing state with a lot of delegates – the idea that there can be any real party unity is over.

For the last several months many Democrats have been amused at the circular firing squad taking place over in the GOP. This has given Democrats hope for November, because history is against them in some respects. After a party has been in the White House for two consecutive terms, voter fatigue is often prevalent, with the desire for something different being more importance than what the change actually is.

This year, all the Republican infighting has turned off much of the electorate and made them more open to what essentially would be Obama's third term. What a stroke of good fortune for Democrats! The Republicans had handed them a gift as their forces would rally behind the steady, measured leadership of Hillary Clinton. That was what was supposed to happen.

The well-heeled Clinton campaign was banking on the idea that, much like the way the electorate responded to Obama in 2008, large swaths of the electorate would be captivated by the opportunity to elect the nation's first woman president. Thus far, the push to get a woman in the White House has been felt by only the most die-hard Clinton supporters. While Mrs. Clinton clearly is the favored candidate of the Democratic Party machine, the energy has clearly been with her opponent, Bernie Sanders. The perplexing question for political junkies observing the Democratic race has been: Was the Sanders phenomenon a testament to the political acumen of a self-described socialist from Vermont? Or was Mrs. Clinton's inability to dispatch Sen. Sanders an ominous red flag about her vulnerabilities as a candidate for the general election?

To borrow a phrase popular among class warriors on the left, Mrs. Clinton was – politically speaking, at least—born on third base. Because of her husband's presidency, she inherited a massive fundraising operation that gave her access to almost limitless funds from high-level donors. Due to a public service career that spanned more than three decades, she enjoys almost universal name recognition. Mrs. Clinton's agenda is the media's agenda—gay rights, female empowerment, income redistribution, universal healthcare, et al—so that she rarely has to confront a hostile press. As

Ted Cruz's satirical television spot said, "It Feels Good to be a Clinton."

Despite all these advantages, turnout is a concern for Team Clinton. Why? The liberal base has been on defense for the last eight years, fending off attacks from the right against Obamacare, immigration policy….basically anything and everything the Obama Administration has advocated. That kind of effort induces a certain weariness. The millennials have gravitated not to Mrs. Clinton but to Sanders, as they have identified him as the candidate with no ties to big banks and corporations. He is the purest socialist to seek the highest office in the land on a major party ticket in almost a century. Fighting a primary process stacked against him, Sanders eventually began attacking Mrs. Clinton for her speeches to Goldman Sachs, her support of the Iraq War and her reluctance to get behind a $15 minimum wage. Mrs. Clinton's campaign is aggressively targeting female millennials in the hopes that they can help with turnout.

Further dampening turnout among the base is the fact that they just don't like her and do not trust her. While many on the left may consider her private email server to be much ado about nothing, they do not feel similarly about her use of the Clinton Foundation as a giant vacuum machine to suck up millions of dollars from the corporate interests that the hard left despises. Despite lack of evidence supporting a "pay-to-play" policy within the State Department, the consistent stream of smoke makes her seem un-credible. Faced with this dilemma, Mrs. Clinton is sure to resort to the same device that got President Obama re-elected in 2012: scare the hell out of the voters about your opponent.

When it comes to public perception, there is little chance altering many people's opinion of Mrs. Clinton. She has been a public figure for more than 30 years, and most people are set in their beliefs about her. She can, however, attempt to place Trump in the most negative light possible. This is one task for which the Democrats excel. Trump can expect to be framed as a racist, xenophobic bigot against Hispanics, a misogynist who can't help but see women as inferior and nothing more than their body parts. Such tactics will be necessary to counter what is widely perceived as an utter lack of charisma and authenticity from Mrs. Clinton.

The other factor that could affect turnout is reconciliation between the primary rivals. Sen. Cruz refused to endorse Mr. Trump at the convention; Gov. Kasich refused to endorse Mr. Trump before the convention as well as refusing to assist in using state GOP resources to help his presidential campaign. There is now open talk of the RNC diverting its resources toward Congressional and other down ballot candidates and letting Mr. Trump free. Mr. Trump has failed to build his own campaign ground game in most of the closest states. If this election is at all close in the swing states, then he will be in huge trouble.

On the other hand, Mrs. Clinton left the Democratic convention with an endorsement from Sen. Sanders and a pledge of support. Mrs. Clinton needs the motivated millennials that pack Sanders rallies. Some of those firebrands have stated publicly that they will never vote for Mrs. Clinton if she is nominated. Add all those elements together and it translates into a campaign that the media can't stop talking about and that Americans have strong opinions about. Turnout, particularly on the Democratic side, may not reach 2008 levels, but the contrasting personalities involved ensure that the campaign will be the number one news topic through November.

CHAPTER EIGHT

PRESIDENTIAL RACE

While Donald Trump and Hillary Clinton represent two of the most well-known candidates to seek the presidency, the big unknown is what will happen when they collide in the general election. More than any other year, the conventional wisdom may not apply to this race. Both candidates have a chance to reshape the electoral map that has become fixed in the last few presidential election cycles. What does each candidate bring to the table to alter politics as usual?

Over the last quarter century, a few trends in electoral politics have become accepted as gospel: The Democrats own the northeastern states; Republicans are hopelessly outnumbered and may as well not even bother to campaign in states like California, Michigan and Massachusetts; and the GOP has a death grip on all the southern states. With this slate of candidates, all of those assumptions could be proven wrong. At the moment, however, Mr. Trump is down in all of the polls nationally, most swing states and in California by 30 points. He is going to have to work hard to recapture his mojo.

Trump is such an unorthodox candidate that he, more so than Mrs. Clinton, is the reason for the contrarian approach to handicapping this race. Your typical Republican presidential nominee from the last few cycles—Mitt Romney or John McCain, to name two—would indeed have trouble winning in those aforementioned Democrat strongholds. Why? The conventional GOP candidate is an easy mark for the Democrats. To them, most Republicans are ripe to be viewed as right-wing extremists, supporters of unpopular wars, and hostile to gay and transgender rights.

This race turns that paradigm on its head. It is the Democrat who is hawkish and talks about nation-building while the Republican candidate talks about the US looking inward, first. Mrs. Clinton is on the record within the last few years stating her position that marriage is between a man and woman. Trump has said in this campaign that transgendered people should use whichever bathroom they want to use. For these and many more reasons, Trump does not fit into the traditional boxes where the Democrats like to put

Republicans. In a year when the electorate on both sides of the political fence are yearning for outsiders, it is the Democrat who comes off as the establishment, party hack with a track record of voting for political expediency. Trump is decidedly non-establishment with mostly conservative policy positions but with a tendency to veer away from conservative orthodoxy when the urge moves him.

If Donald Trump can get out of his own way so that he can bring the focus back to the public's lack of trust in Hillary Clinton, he has the opportunity to dig himself out of the deep hole that he's dug.

Negative campaigning works. In 2012, the Obama campaign took an opponent who was relatively unknown nationally and were able to frame him as a one-percenter, a fabulously wealthy financier who ruthlessly closed businesses and cost people their jobs. Was that characterization true? Probably not, but Romney was not aggressive enough or quick enough on his feet to respond to the charges and put the Obama campaign on the defensive about his first term where his record was spotty at best. If Romney was ruthless in business, it did not cross over to the political realm and President Obama was re-elected by a comfortable margin.

Those who think Trump will allow himself to be similarly portrayed are in for a shock. While Romney's handlers mostly had him in front of a teleprompter to avoid gaffes, until recently Trump has proven to be immune to gaffes. He is more comfortable in a stream-of-consciousness style and says whatever he thinks at a given moment: Let Trump be Trump. Lately, however, his frequent gaffes and petty feuds have lost traction with the voters. Will the change in his campaign leadership be enough to get him to focus on Mrs. Clinton's deficits or will he continue to allow the mainstream media to ignore her flaws. We know one thing for certain. He will go for the jugular on his opponent in a way that few Republicans ever have. For many years the Democrats were willing and able to go negative against their GOP opponents with the confidence that said opponent would play by Marquis of Queensbury rules while they were willing to go no-hold-barred.

This time will be different. Trump will use scorched earth tactics against Mrs. Clinton, bringing up many of her scandals that no politician before has mentioned. Mrs. Clinton is not used to facing an opponent willing to do that, and the potential exists for many cringe-worthy moments when they debate. Mrs. Clinton will be the one in this race who is programmed and uncomfortable going off script. Look for Trump to try and push her buttons to make her look flustered and on the defensive.

Don't think, however, that Mrs. Clinton is without her own weaponry. What she lacks in likability and speaking style, she will compensate with the strength of her political machine. Chief among her assets will be the mainstream media. While the fourth estate has been riding the Trump bandwagon for high ratings during the primaries, their tone will change dramatically when the candidates pivot to the general election.

In 2008 John McCain was the darling of the media. "The Maverick," as they dubbed him, commanded respect as a survivor of the Hanoi Hilton and had the wisdom and experience of his long tenure in Washington. At least that was the narrative when he was running in the GOP primaries. Fast forward to 2008 when his opponent in the general election was Senator Barack Obama, the media view of Sen. McCain changed altogether. Now he was seen as a dinosaur, a relic from the past standing in the way of the historic election of the nation's first African-American president. Like Mr. Romney, Sen. McCain lacked the charisma, aggressiveness and oratory skills to counter the barrage.

Perhaps because of its loyal constituencies among blacks, women and lower income voters, Democrats in previous campaign have had success framing their Republican opponents as hostile to those groups. Mrs. Clinton's campaign will also be ready and willing to use these strategies against Trump. His provocative comments about Mexican illegal immigrants are tailor-made for this attack. Team Hillary will run his comments *ad nauseam* and convince Hispanic Americans that he wants all of them deported. As Trump ramps up his attacks on Hillary, she will no doubt accuse him of being hostile to women in general. Trump has a long record of comments on women's appearances that will provide attack ad fodder. Mrs. Clinton will also benefit from the Democratic Party's most loyal constituency—black voters—who will reliably pull the lever for the Democrat even if they have no particular love for her.

Because Trump is a lifelong resident of New York state and perhaps its most well-known citizen, he will likely fare better there and in the surrounding states than the typical Republican. But can he actually win there against the entrenched Democrat machine and its constituencies? It is impossible to know, but expect him to actually compete in those states where his predecessors may have been quick to write them off.

Conversely, Trump may not have a lock on states that have been traditionally Republican. The flip-side of Trump's unconventional appeal is that conservative voters may not view him as one of them. The GOP primaries were uncharacteristically nasty, with Trump hurling personal invective against almost all of his opponents. Would supporters of Ted Cruz, Marco Rubio and Jeb Bush be willing to bury the hatchet and vote for Trump? The short answer is no. The larger question is whether or not it will ultimately matter.

Another question of Trump's national strategy is whether the Republican National Committee (RNC) will throw its resources behind him. During primary season Trump seemed perpetually at odds with the RNC. After getting his signature on a pledge to not run a third-party campaign, the party leaders drew criticism from Trump for the delegate system that saw Cruz win races where no votes were cast. For weeks the media was titillated by reports that the RNC was considering nominating a hand-picked candidate like Speaker of the House Paul Ryan rather than Trump. Obviously the RNC abandoned that movement but it remains unclear whether or not they will continue to support Mr. Trump throughout the general election campaign. There is a growing chorus from the Republican establishment calling for a focus on down ballot races with the Senate and House now in jeopardy.

After his lopsided win in the Indiana primary on April 4, a number of conventional wisdoms were laid to rest. The GOP convention will be contested! Wrong. Trump is a fad that will go away by the spring! Wrong. The establishment will rally and find a way to deny Trump the nomination! Wrong again. By vanquishing his remaining competition in Cruz and John Kasich, Trump did what few thought he could do: enter the presidential race as a complete political novice and win a major party nomination. As wild and contentious as the primaries have been, Trump vs. Clinton promises to be a race unlike any the American voting public has ever seen.

CHAPTER NINE

HEADING TO THE POLLS

It is daunting to write a book on the upcoming general election because it is so completely unpredictable and ever-evolving. It is a campaign that will hinge on the answers to a few critical questions. Among them: Will Mr. Trump's one-man publicity-generating machine and shoestring budget campaign be enough to overcome Mrs. Clinton's extensive fund-raising and get-out-the-vote apparatus? Will Mr. Trump be able to control his P.T. Barnum-like impulses long enough to reassure the electorate that he can be President? Will the press eschew Mr. Trump's wild ride and focus on Mrs. Clinton's flaws as a candidate and potential President?

As he had promised, Trump is pulling no punches in his attacks on Mrs. Clinton. He has gone where no opponent has ever gone before, bringing up the Juanita Broaddrick rape allegation against President Clinton that was summarily dismissed by the political media decades ago. While Trump supporters have relished the attacks, he is walking a fine line with this strategy. If done just right, it could serve to expose skeletons in the Clintons' past that younger generations may know little about. While the affairs were minimized by Clinton backers in the 90's—"it's only sex"—millennial women are far more sensitive to allegations of sexual harassment and may have a very different reaction. If done crudely and excessively, Trump attacks could appear like he is piling on to a scorned wife and generate sympathy for Mrs. Clinton; worse yet, Mr. Trump's attacks open himself to a similar debate.

Team Hillary has come out with a narrative that Trump is a "loose cannon" who cannot be trusted with the economic, military and cultural keys to the kingdom. If the Trump *id* is released on the campaign trail, it will give ammunition to that claim. There is little evidence that Trump can be managed by handlers. Former Trump *consigliere* Paul Manafort—a longtime Washington political insider—had reportedly urged Trump to tone down his rhetoric, and even assured a group of GOP leaders that Trump's schtick on the trail was exactly that.

Trump responded by marginalizing Manafort (who quickly resigned) and added Breitbart executive Stephen Bannon as the campaign's CEO and Kellyanne Conway to run the day-to-day operations. Given that his popularity surged by simply being himself early in the campaign, the question may not be whether Trump will listen to his handlers' advice, but should he? A watered-down Trump may not have the same appeal to those who waited in long lines to attend his rallies and see him as a change agent in Washington. Bannon firmly believes in former Trump campaign manager, Cori Lewandowski's strategy of "Let Trump be Trump," so it remains to be seen which campaign is going to emerge.

American voters are a fickle bunch with a short attention span. Rarely do they award the White House to any political party for more than two consecutive terms. Mrs. Clinton's value proposition is that she is essentially promising a third Obama term. Even those who may have a favorable opinion of President Obama may be looking for change in Washington after eight years. Every administration reaches a point in its second term where it appears to be out of dynamic ideas and is limping toward the finish line. The challenge for Mrs. Clinton will be to repackage that proposition as something to get excited about, because without the proper framing it looks like an unimaginative extension of the status quo.

Trump, no matter what people think of him, is clearly the candidate promising to bring change. He would be a dramatic departure from the leadership style and vision of the incumbent. The human desire for something new could work to his advantage. When presented with the choice of the same thing versus something new, even if the new thing might be considered risky, there is a percentage of the population that will go for the new option. Trump is betting on this.

It has been widely reported in media campaign coverage that Trump has a problem with women and Hispanics. That is true, as his style and policy proposals are not necessarily tailored to those groups. There are two other factors that are under-reported or not reported at all. What Trump appears to be losing with women and minorities, he seems to be making up with a broader cross-section of white males. Among them are the modern incarnation of the "Reagan Democrats" that launched Ronald Reagan to power in 1980.

While the Democrats have secured their grip on women and minorities over the last few election cycles, they have alienated large swaths of white males who feel excluded by the Democratic platform. Such men, particularly those in blue-collar jobs, have gravitated to Trump's message of smarter trade deals, more jobs and an immigration policies that includes enforcement of borders. An example of this was seen in the West Virginia primaries.

West Virginia has been a reliable blue state since the 1980s. Mrs. Clinton made a political faux pas in March by proclaiming that she was going to "put a lot of coal miners and coal companies out of business." That statement unquestionably contributed to Mrs. Clinton losing the West Virginia primary to Bernie Sanders. Seizing on the opening, Trump appeared in West Virginia and promised to get coal miners back to work if elected. The move resulted in Trump getting the endorsement of the West Virginia Coal Association. Without a whole lot of effort, Trump had accomplished what the national GOP has failed to do as of late: turn a traditional Democratic-held state from blue to red.

The other factor is Mrs. Clinton's inverse problem. She is strong with minorities and women, and weak with white males. This may have been the reason for Mrs. Clinton's surprising announcement that she would put her husband in charge of managing the nation's economy if elected. Like most political calculations, this move is a gamble with significant risks. Bill is undeniably more popular than his wife. Seeing Mr. Clinton as an active player in a Clinton Administration—with memories of a booming economy in the 90s—may help her bridge the gender gap. The danger is that she risks alienating some of her female support. The central theme of her campaign is that she will be an empowered, decisive woman in the White House. That image may be diminished by a perception that she needs a man—her husband, no less—to tackle one of the central responsibilities of the presidency.

Predictions? There are none forthcoming for what has thus far been the most unpredictable campaign that almost anyone can remember. But this much is certain: it will be the political equivalent of a spectacular train wreck, a big noisy, ugly spectacle. And none of us will be able to look away from it.

CHAPTER TEN

THE FINAL SHOWDOWN

Since the end of primary season, the campaign has been highlighted mostly by the candidates' shortcomings. Donald Trump's lack of organization and political machinery has led to some avoidable mistakes. During the GOP convention, some very effective speeches were obscured by controversy over whether portions of Melania Trump's speech were lifted from Michelle Obama's 2008 convention speech. A seasoned corps of speechwriters and handlers would likely have nipped such a problem in the bud, but without that kind of oversight it became a media theme for the duration of the convention.

Similarly, Hillary Clinton's post-primary performance may have raised more questions than it has answered. FBI Director James Comey's much anticipated announcement that he would not recommend prosecution of Clinton for her email server must have generated a huge sigh of relief at Clinton headquarters in Brooklyn, but reports that Bill Clinton had a secret meeting with Attorney General Loretta Lynch created a perception that a backroom deal had been struck. Rather than address the matter comprehensively, Mrs. Clinton has decided to abstain from press conferences and apparently run out the clock on the email issue.

After the GOP convention in Cleveland, Trump supporters hoped their candidate would pivot into a more presidential mode that would win over undecided voters. What followed was several weeks of Trump getting lost in the proverbial weeds, engaging in media-generated controversies involving a Hispanic judge presiding over his Trump University lawsuit and disparaging comments about the Muslim Gold Star family that spoke at the Democratic Convention. A virtual tie in the polls after the GOP convention turned into what looked like an insurmountable Clinton lead. The result was a shakeup of Trump's campaign leadership, with Paul Manafort being sacked and replaced with Breitbart.com boss Steven Bannon and pollster Kellyanne Conway. The result has been a more focused Trump who reads speeches off a teleprompter and does less stream of consciousness speaking.

With Mrs. Clinton's legal problems regarding the email server behind her, focus has now turned to her dealings with the Clinton Foundation during her time as secretary of state. Wikileaks editor Julian Assange released emails and the Associated Press wrote a story that suggested a pay-for-play culture at the Clinton State Department where more than half of Mrs. Clinton's meetings were with high-dollar Foundation donors. If such revelations have hurt Mrs. Clinton, they have not been seen in the polls at the time of this writing. Still, Clinton supporters are likely to be on edge until the election, worried that a bombshell disclosure on with the emails or the Clinton Foundation could tip the scales of the election.

Everything that has happened thus far has to be seen through the prism of the summer. During that time, the attention of much of the electorate is on kids and summer vacations. It is only after Labor Day that most Americans pay close attention to their choice of candidates. By this measure, the importance of the three scheduled debates cannot be overstated. It will be the best chance for voters to see Trump and Mrs. Clinton in an unscripted environment, the two candidates exchanging fire face-to-face.

The pressure on the candidates in the debates is exorbitant because of the high-possibility for a campaign-changing gaffe.

Mrs. Clinton has a habit of looking stiff and uncomfortable in the debate format. Trump is more comfortable in front of cameras, but has a maddening habit of going off message and saying things his staffers have to explain to the press the next day. Because of the Roman Colosseum quality for the debates, they are likely to garner Super Bowl-sized ratings.

In the final analysis, each candidate is playing their opponents, characterization of them. Part of Trump's message is that Mrs. Clinton represents the status quo, the inside the Beltway establishment that has caused many voters to believe the nation is on the wrong track. Mrs. Clinton is embracing the perception that she is a symbol of Washington, but only in the sense that she is a steady, experienced hand who will draw upon her experience to deliver measured leadership.

Mrs. Clinton's primary point of attack against Trump is that he is a loose cannon, a possibly psychopathic megalomaniac who is unfit to be untrusted with the nuclear codes. Trump seems to relish the idea of the outsider, something the voters have never seen before. He is banking that the country is tired of career politicians and, in a state of despair after several difficult years of war, terrorism and economic stagnation, will turn to someone who has no hand in creating the current mess.

What will happen next is impossible to predict, because quite simply there has never been a series of events like the ones we have seen this political season. Given the choices facing the next president, the only certainty is that the decision made this November will be one that will change the course of the nation for decades and beyond.

VIDEO CONTENT

CHAPTER THREE

1. Hillary campaign launch quote. https://www.youtube. com/watch?v=-i8vdM15K6c
2. Bill Clinton "Era of Big Government is over." https:// www.youtube.com/watch?v=P5eyI5r2j2c
3. Hillary Clinton says she'll put Bill 'in charge' of fixing economy. http://money.cnn.com/2016/05/16/news/ economy/hillary-bill-clinton-economic-job-growth/
4. HIllary- "I'm no Tammy Wynette." https://www. youtube.com/watch?v=NULkwDWjbmc

CHAPTER FOUR

1. Reagan ad; Morning in America. https://www.youtube. com/watch?v=EU-IBF8nwSY
2. Trump comment "Rosie O'Donnell is a fat pig." https://www.youtube.com/watch?v=0zt3Ic11H6Q

CHAPTER FIVE

1. 1960 presidential debate. https://www.youtube.com/watch?v=gbrcRKqLSRw
2. Trump attacks Rand Paul. https://www.youtube.com/watch?v=LrE9Roa8028
3. Sanders sick of Clinton's emails. https://www.youtube.com/watch?v=aOOfwN0iYxM

CHAPTER SIX

1. Trump: Clinton is not a victim. https://www.youtube.com/watch?v=rxGTCcqmcu4
2. Hillary Clinton, security review. https://www.youtube.com/watch?v=G2G-D4pRUKw
3. James Comey will not recommend prosecution. https://www.youtube.com/watch?v=ghph_361wa0
4. Donald Trump, "they're rapists." https://www.youtube.com/watch?v=C6QEqoYgQxw
5. Ivana Trump felt "violated." http://www.thedailybeast.com/articles/2015/07/27/ex-wife-donald-trump-made-feel-violated-during-sex.html

CHAPTER SEVEN

1. Feels good to be a Clinton. https://www.youtube.com/ watch?v=FECIYlo3KRY

CHAPTER NINE

1. Juanita Broaddrick. http://www.wnd.com/2016/05/ broaddrick-on-evil-clinton-rape-i-could-never-forgive-them/